Wore Down Trust

WORE DOWN TRUST

a blues in three lives

Michael Blouin

PEDLAR PRESS | Toronto

COPYRIGHT © 2011 Michael Blouin

ALL RIGHTS RESERVED. No part of this book may be reproduced or transmitted in any form or by any means whatsoever without written permission from the publisher, except by a reviewer, who may quote brief passages in a review. For information, write Pedlar Press at PO Box 26, Station P, Toronto Ontario M5S 2S6 Canada.

ACKNOWLEDGEMENTS
The publisher wishes to thank the Canada Council for the Arts and the Ontario Arts Council for their generous support of our publishing program.

LIBRARY AND ARCHIVES CANADA
CATALOGUING IN PUBLICATION

Blouin, Michael, 1960-
    Wore down trust / Michael Blouin.

Poems.

ISBN 978-1-897141-40-3

    I. Title.

PS8603.L69W67 2011   C811'.6
C2011-901088-7

BOOK DESIGN
Zab Design & Typography, Toronto

TYPEFACE
Memphis

Printed in Canada

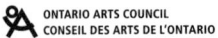

for David Katulski

THE PLAYERS

JOHNNY CASH was born into rural poverty in an out-of-the-way place in the first half of the last century his father working the sawmill or clearing land for low wages. Johnny struggled to make ends meet while embarking on a career in the arts, which, though a struggle at first, would eventually bring him notoriety and success, a wide and appreciative audience, accolades and awards. The love of a good woman in large part saved him from his own excesses. His empathy for the common man as well as his own working-class origins were evident themes throughout his work as were the dependencies that troubled him. He met Alden Nowlan in Fredericton in May of 1975. He died sooner than many would have preferred, leaving behind a rich body of work.

ALDEN NOWLAN was born into rural poverty in an out-of-the-way place in the first half of the last century his father working the saw mill or clearing land for low wages. Alden struggled to make ends meet while embarking on a career in the arts, which, though a struggle at first, would eventually bring him notoriety and success, a wide and appreciative audience, accolades and awards. The love of a good woman in large part saved him from his own excesses. His empathy for the common man as well as his own working-class origins were evident themes throughout his work as were the dependencies that troubled him. He met Johnny Cash in Fredericton in May of 1975. He died sooner than many would have preferred, leaving behind a rich body of work.

THE AUTHOR was born. Most things end in darkness. Not everything. Not everything dies.

JOHNNY

June	wife
Carrie	mother
Jack	brother
John Carter	son
Roseanne	daughter
Kristoferson	Kris Kristoferson, friend, musician
Luther Perkins	musician, friend

ALDEN

Claudine	wife
Grace	mother
Fred Cogswell	friend
Johnnie	stepson
Harriet	sister
Layton	Irving Layton, friend, poet
Elizabeth Brewster	poet, friend

THE AUTHOR

Will insist on interjecting in distracting ways serving the same purpose as the third bar in traditional blues.

ON THE POEMS AND PLAYERS
Except where obvious or as indicated as excerpts
of personal letters, songs or poems, the voices here are imagined.
But hopefully none the less real for that.

Most things border the truth.

A   Country music is soul music I think. Poetry. It all comes from the
    same place. Way down. When I'm on stage I'm not anywhere else.

A   It's always pulling on me though, this dark. I think it pulls on a lot
    of people. I don't wish it to pull me away.

B   Johnny once stayed with some of my wife's people for a few days.
    They said he was just as nice and as genuine as he seemed.

THIS RECORD is for anyone who's been broken. And
been healed. Or is waiting.

It is difficult to determine the specific origins of the blues. There is some agreement that the early development of the form was heavily influenced by work songs or "field hollers" of the rural south. The structure of the blues is unique. The distinguishing twelve-bar AAB pattern is restricted to the use of only three chords. In the three sets of four bars of the twelve-bar blues the second four bars repeat the first, with a slight lyrical or tonal variation, and the third bar is something different which expands the lyrical theme and returns the pattern to its origins.

I went to the crossroad, fell down on my knee,
Went to the crossroad, fell down on my knee,
Asked the Lord above to have mercy, save poor Bob if you please.

"Crossroad Blues," on *Robert Johnson: King of the Delta Blues* Columbia CL 30034

This basic pattern is easily modified for variation. The structure is simple and the repetition has a reassuring quality.

Oh, admit this, man, there is no point in poetry
if you withhold the truth
once you've come by it.
– ALDEN NOWLAN

I got to keep moving, I got to keep moving
Blues falling down like hail, blues falling down like hail.
– ROBERT JOHNSON, "Hellhound on My Trail"

If only the wind carried the clouds back
If only his failures added up to pride.
– SANDRA RIDLEY, *Lift – Ghazals for C*

JOHNNY

WORE DOWN TRUST BLUES

A   Kind of faith June has for me 'bout wore down to nothing
kind of faith June has for me 'bout wore down to nothing by now
but like the rock in the unfarmed field it's not going anywhere.

A   It's been a very long time in coming this peace that I feel in the mornings now that we have returned to Hickory Lake. I keep telling people that this is all I want, that this somehow makes all of it worth the doing and the living through. And they smile as though what I'm saying makes some sort of sense to them. But for most of them, I think, it does not. I can tell by the look in their eyes when I use words like redemption and salvation. They either get it or they do not. There's not one of them, though, whom I do not wish well, for whom I do not wish the very best.

I know what it is to not be where I am now. I'm not forgetting that.

B   This house is dark. Just enough light to tear faded patterns on yellowing wallpaper. Hobos pass by. Nothing predictable about a dead man. When Johnny shows up at my door, there is no one more surprised than me. First of all he's dead. Second, and this is important; he's pissed. It's a hot night. Shimmers of heat in the air. He asks for a glass of water. It seems a simple enough request. At first.

Aside from God, I'm the only thing I'm afraid of.

When you can find it, truth sings.

A   Now this is the whole thing
and there's no point in going on about it
or dressing it all up somehow.

The thing is I was saved.
He came down and He picked me right up –
it shines the way that it is –

I guess that with some things there's no point
in having them be anything
but just plain simple.

A   When I was down in that hole there was nothing going to bring me up,
Down in that hole there was nothing that was going to bring me up.
Nothing that I knew. Not any sympathy. Walking down the road.
But going nowhere.

B   Took something beyond what I knew to do. It took accepting love. I had to be taught that. And a lesson like that. Not easy.

A   Some of the first music I remember hearing I guess would be field hollers, which was maybe a simple kind of blues, and it was a spiritual kind of singing that went back and forth in the cotton fields. It was calling to each other; it was saying "I'm still here." It was music as a way of getting through which I think is still an important part of what music is. For a good number of people anyway. There's all kinds of cotton fields, all kinds of disappointment. It's a way to just get through.

A   I Am Bound For The Promised Land

     That was, I believe, the first song I ever sung,
     at least it's the first one I have a memory of singing.
     I was in the back of a flatbed truck
     on the way to our second house in Dyess –
     sometimes my Mother would sing
     and sometimes she'd cry
     and sometimes you couldn't tell which.
     Us kids would all be in the back
     and we'd pull over to the side of the mud road at night
     in that government truck –
     there were heavy rains that spring
     and we'd just have an old tarp
     and our bodies were heavy
     the weight of that tiredness you know
     crept over you like rising cotton –
     and I remember having this sense
     at that age

that when I was singing
I knew what I was doing,
folks stopped what they were doing and they listened.

I was puny though,
not strong or smart like Jack
who was going to be a preacher.

When I sang folks looked at me like they would a talking dog,
admiration there, sure
but some pity too.

B   J.R. empties the glass. Holds it in his hand and looks at it. Eyes closed and then a thought. Sets it down careful. The last few nights I have slept in the heat upstairs turning in dreams that give me no rest. Midnight blood turning dark. Moths hover by the porch light. I see the wrong I've done. See it clear. But when you're in a prison you don't look up.

A The people we had to see were down in the hollow. We had worked most of that day in the fields and then done some work inside replacing a rotten sill. The sun was so hot you'd still feel it on your skin after you went to bed. Night sun. We came up over a rise and I saw the distance of where we were going.

Jack had a preserve jar full of tea tied to his belt and we'd have to make that last. There was no sugar to be had so the taste of the tea was bitter but it worked on the thirst. Daddy had a lot but one thing he didn't have was money so sugar wasn't something we saw a lot of. I didn't mind the walking – a man's got to have time to think, I told myself. I think I would have been six. This was after we moved to Dyess. Jack got his job working Saturdays at the high school agricultural shop cutting oak trees into fence posts. Jack turned over all his money to Mother.

The loudest sound in Kingsland County, aside from the train and the mill, was the water in the creek near our house. It made you feel some cooler just to hear it. There were good fish in there too. We didn't get a lot of time to fish but those times make up some of the happiest memories I have of my childhood. We kept on, down past the churches and the pond and around past the feed mill and the general store.

We passed a farm where some boys were taking potshots at a Dr. Pepper bottle on a fence. It didn't look to me like they'd ever hit it. We were walking all that way because we owed money to a man in the hollow and not having any money to give him we were carrying a bale of fair to middlin' cotton between us as a down payment. It was hot carryin' weather, which I guess is why

I remember it so well. I remember my Daddy sayin' the man was all gravy with no bread meaning I think he had money but no sense.

It's funny the things that stick with you.

My people originally hailed from Ireland, descended from King Duff. The motto on my people's coat of arms was " Better Times Will Come."

Much of the time though, they did not.

I miss my brother.

A   The first house didn't have any windows,
    she hung blankets –

    she hung blankets, whatever she could find
    they made the best they could

    she hung blankets – they made their way the best they could
    you could find her heart on any map, the soft breeze not stirring.

B   I don't think anyone who hasn't had demons
could possibly know what it's like to have them.

I don't see how they could.

Hell hounds.

I have stayed in this house for lack of other places. It looks like the home of Huck Finn at forty-nine, the home of a young boy allowed to smoke cigarettes and drink whisky. We all have ghosts. It's not so important what they are. It's that we have them. I'm telling you. They rattle around here like they own the place. And they don't. They don't. You don't have what you want, they mutter. They shift furniture in the dark.

I have seen the face of death and let me tell you this. It accepts. In the end, it accepts.

A   We used to swim, Jack and I, in the creek
and we'd jump together into the cool water
and
this is what I wanted to tell you –
every time I came back up to the surface
it was a surprise.

A   Mornings I wake up now and all I want is coffee. Maybe I want some eggs too. On a wild occasion I will have a biscuit or two. I lie in for a while, enjoying the fact that I will not be up soon searching in last night's pockets for pills, under the bed for bottles. I listen to the sounds of the ice cracking in the pond, snow coming down off the roof. I'm saying now that I rejoice. I reach for June not to have her, but to hold her.

There's a world of understanding in the difference.

There's having a gun and there's using it. There's the Gospel. And there's living.

B   When you find the truth you don't put that down again. God help you if you do. You'll have the devil to pay. But the Lord loves a sinner. Loves a soul in tears.

When you can find it, truth sings.

A   Jack's in the barn,
out of the sun for now,
we're drying the peanuts from our fields,
picking out the ones we won't use
then the ones ready for roasting.
We get brown paper sacks from the co-op
and we'll sell them outside the theatre tonight in Dyess,
a hot June night –
girls in their dresses and the June bugs –
a nickel for a small bag,
for a big one a dime.

A   I used to think Jack had everything that was good between the two of us, and that when he was taken, all of the good was just gone out of me. I still think that's mostly true, but I can live now without having to hide it all of the time. Without having to run. You see, I'm telling you. I'm telling you now. It's not a secret anymore – to anyone else or to me.

That creek not too far from the house in Dyess. Sometimes we went there together to fish and it was wonderful. Those are some of the happiest memories I have. Some of the best moments I've ever had. And there were times I went there alone. Those times were different. I knew, even then.

B   I'll tell you one story, the most run-of-the-mill one; it was July, I'm fairly certain and it was dripping heat. We were living in a hundred-year-old house in Eastern Ontario. I loved that house, which was haunted I think although I never saw anything except out of the corner of my eye. I remember the old wallpaper shredded and in piles in the corners. I remember the cold smell of the cistern. I heard things. Voices. Other people saw things, saw people and they've told me about it and I believe them. These are not people given to exaggeration or to the fabrication of lies. That's me.

This day I was at the top of a twenty-five-foot extension ladder just under the eaves where there was a little shade. Not that it helped any. It was rattlesnake hot – the kind of heat that buzzes in your head. I was scraping thirty-year-old paint from hundred-year-old wood but having a fine time not thinking of much. I have friends who know a lot about electricity. I've done a little wiring myself – nothing fancy. I have friends who've been nearly abducted by serial killers, who've survived terrorist explosions, who've seen buddies skinned alive in war, who've sized up cancer and found it wanting. I've been attacked with a knife, I've pulled a suicide out of the path of a truck, fallen twenty feet to concrete in a bar fight, lost two thirds of my blood, I've been taken down at gun point, had loaded guns at the back of my head – no safety – rolled a Jeep, been airlifted out. "He may not make it."

The wires coming into the house at the eave weren't grounded. As I said, it was an old house. Things loosen over time.

But I'm still here. I've lost touch with a lot of people I've known. I say almost died or been killed eight times. I don't really know how many more there might be. They say 220 volts is enough to kill you. Certainly the wrong landing off a twenty-five-foot fall might. Barroom fight, push through a railing, twenty-foot fall to concrete might. A good rollover might. A head-on might. A knife might. A gun would. A gun to the back of the head would. A loose finger. A finger too tight. Look there's been a lot of poems written about this let me just make it simple. The car won't start and she left me this morning. Her cup of coffee is still sitting warm on the counter.

A   My mother made us better
than we were.

She had a plastic barrette for her hair that was black and silver and she kept it careful so the silver wouldn't come off and it would always look real. It was the only pretty thing our family had.

A   Her people were made of stern stuff. They say that steel is strong because it knew the hammer and that is true when it comes to my mother and where it came to her people. Some folks are born stronger and mostly they're the ones have to spend their lives proving it. In poverty the tests come early and they don't waver. Something about being poor is that it's persistent. Poverty is patient and tenacious and my mother knew all about that, understood the rock in the field too heavy to move. Most times she just out-patiented it. She taught us to do that too. Hard work never hurt anyone and it kept us from starving to death. But I had something in me that wasn't in her. It just wasn't there as far as I could see, like a need to not do right. A hunger for it. She'd call that selfish, I guess. She'd call it the devil. And I guess she'd be right, she was about most things. There's a story told about the great bluesman Howlin' Wolf. His momma was a God-fearing woman and when he returned years later to Mississippi to try to give her some money she just threw it back at him and told him she wouldn't take money that's been got playin' the devil's music. Blind Willie Johnson his momma threw lye in his face that's what they say. I remember my own mother saying, "John you just shake that or you'll come to no good." And I did certain enough. I did.

And I don't mean that I shook it. I came to more than my share of no good, more than most people's share. My cup ran over with it.

June changed all that. The grace of the Lord changed that.

B   Each at the top of his own ladder. Waiting. Ghosts.

A   When the picking was done
you'd take your cotton to the gin
and the fella there'd take out his little notebook
and he'd dig into your bale
and he'd make his little note about the quality of your cotton
and he'd rip the page out and stick it on your bale
and that's how much you'd get for your crop
the grades, if I remember,
were Strict High Middlin'
High Middlin'
Fair to Middlin'
Middlin'
Low Middlin'
and there was
Strict Low Middlin'

A   June never placed herself above anyone else in this world,
never placed herself above anyone,
she was just there, Strict High Middlin'.

B   When I was a boy I had moments of calm patience and I see them now like the sun over a field. When I was twenty-six I lost most of the blood in my body on a warm July Sunday. It pooled bright around me like the morning light in a mirror. God had got tired of waiting, you see. He didn't leave me any other option. He knew I couldn't see very well on my own. He had to open me right up just to show me.

Picked me up. Set me down.

I've come to look at writing now like conjuring. Poetry like a card trick that you perform on the street or in a bar, walking right up to the stranger's face and producing the ace of spades in front of them like it came from nowhere. From nothing. There. See what I've done? The ace of spades – bet you weren't expecting that – I hope you weren't expecting that.

The novel is more like a big stage trick; sawing a lady in half maybe. It's a bigger trick. It requires more time and preparation. More practice. There's going to be some equipment involved. Some lifting.

I don't know what this is. This is something else. I sit with paper, the moon shifting across the floor, my bones adjusting. Write it down.

As I said, it seemed to me like he was pissed. He set the glass down careful. Baleful eyes.

"Let me ask you something," he said "what is it that you're waiting for?"

I thought he meant I should ask him in off the porch out of the night. No. He didn't.

A   Above the stove
       she saw
       black earth cotton field
       through the dirty window
       she saw
       her boys
       coffee pot
       chipped blue enamel
       a bible

       She saw a bible
       cut trunks of trees
       the little porch
       unpainted

A   What I Saw

       My brother's blood dirty clothes on the top of a rain barrel
       my father crying

       first and last

B   I can't tell you too much about dying. I can speak to you about not dying. I have become a small-time expert on that. I can speak with some authority on a number of things like small-time experts do. On my upper arm I have a tattoo that says "saved" and on the other arm it says "trust." Each one has its meaning and each its purpose. Mostly, though, they're about remembering. Really, they're about not forgetting. The fact that it could all pass without having been remarked on. Scares me. That each day I wake up on the right side of the grass. And one day, won't. On my right forearm it says "know who you owe." I wanted to be reminded. All the time. Each day a new one. Each day another.

A   Jack leaves by dying.
Several crows watch from the telephone wires
the small dug grave.
How can I go on from here?
Bruised and scraped
and cut and burned
thoughts flung far over the fields
shadows on the wallpaper
the hungry unquestioning blade
that sliced him through
severed his clean body
stopped only when it was
far too late
his government issue shirt and pants
drenched –
such a small grave.

I'm glad you're all here
he said
terrible eyes
sawdust voice.
It's a beautiful river Mamma, can you see it?
Then he coughed up
all that was in him.

The box slowly covered
the crows out low over the cotton.
How can I go on from here?
No other friend.
There
that says it.

A   When Jack left us I didn't know much about much. I didn't know about holes. The ways they can be filled.

B   I asked him in. Asked him if he'd like to have a seat. Who knows if a dead man has a need to sit down? It seemed for a minute as if he didn't know. He looked around slowly as if it was a complicated question. His eyes passed over the couch and leather chairs of the living room and lit upon the plain wooden chair in the kitchen.

"Yes," he said then, "…yes, I believe I would."

He looked at his hands on the table in the light and then he began to speak. He kept right on speaking for quite some time. It's a long walk home. And you never get there.

A   The day after Jack's funeral we were all of us back in the fields and it was blinding. Ten hours of chopping weeds from the cotton. My mother dropped to her knees finally in the dirt. My poor daddy tried to take her arm to help her up but she yelled at him.

"I'll get up when *God pushes* me up!"

Which I guess He did just a few crying moments later because she took herself up and she went back to the cutting. June bugs hovering. Sweat in our eyes.

A   You're reaching out for something and you oughta be reaching up. That's the problem. Out, you're only going to find more trouble. Out, there's only more like you.

B   When I say that I've been lifted up, and I am saying that – we might as well be clear about that from the outset – I don't mean to say that I've been lifted higher than anyone else.

You have to remember.

I was pretty far down to start.

A   I see him sometimes
      Jack
      in my dreams
      and he's a preacher
      just like he always said he would be
      and he treats the Lord's words
      with such care.

A   The crows lift from the fields. A conspiracy of wings.

B   I pray three times a day. It's nothing to boast about. Knees on these floorboards. I'm trying to live up to something I've been given. In that sense I am proud.

A   He isn't really gone
      Jack has stayed with me
      he's there
      in the songs we sang
      at his funeral
      Peace in the Valley
      I'll Fly Away
      How Beautiful Heaven Must Be…
      all of them
      wherever I go
      I can start singing one of them
      and I begin to feel peace
      at times they've been my only way back
      from the bad places the black dog
      calls home.

      We have to sing
      it's one of the ways
      we keep God alive.

A   I couldn't sell appliances – didn't care whether people wanted 'em or not. The fellow I worked for, who was nice enough to give me a job and to keep me at it long after he must have realized I was no value to him, said, "John you have to sell yourself, not the machine." I do that some I guess – selling myself, but not the way so there's none left.

      Selling Cash.

But keeping Johnny.

You're not selling the machine. I just didn't mind if Mrs. Smith bought a washing machine or didn't buy a washing machine, even if it did mean food on my table. It didn't mean food as if I'd grown it myself with my hands and it didn't mean anything like selling a song. I'd have played for free though. Did play for free. Played the back of a flatbed truck. Store openings. My shoulders aching.

B   Into my own mirror. Wake up feeling like I've been put in a bag and beaten with hammers. Again.

I've been given a prescription for antidepressants. I can't say that I've ever used it. I've used other things instead. Can I say that? Yes. I can say that. I kept that piece of paper in my wallet for months. Felt better when I got rid of it.

Cash and I sit at the kitchen table in this house that was built out of stone and tree trunks over a hundred and fifty years ago by farm people. There is nothing in the original structure that is not simply made. And I want to tell Cash this. There is nothing in my life that I have not complicated. Want to tell him this too. This I know he would understand. What we share.

Eggs and cigarettes for breakfast. Cash doesn't eat. Smokes incessantly.

The women I've loved have loved me back. I can't help that.

Seven guns pointed at me at once. I want to tell him this too. He stares at his hands as if they belong to someone else. As if they were a question. We talk about guns a bit and Cash knows a lot about guns from hunting wild turkey mostly. I tell him I'd like to hunt.

"I can tell you this," he says, eyeing me across the table, "in the things we want, there is usually much that we do not know…"

Close my eyes. Then.

A One time I asked my friend the doctor
if he had something for the times I just sat in the car
parked
staring
if he had something for brokenness.
He said "J.R., there's no pill cures that."

I asked him if he had something for silence
something easier to swallow
than these pills I take.
I lifted my head
turned and coughed
something for the edginess
and sharp corners
something for attachment.
Loosened my shirt
took a deep breath
something quiet
and discrete
indiscernible
to the human eye.

Asked him about joy
and damnation
pain, and no pain –

opened my mouth –

he gave me a prescription
one of the big ones, I recognized the name
said the side effects are minimal.

Wait, I have it here.
No
I've lost it.

Sometimes we're broken
hands searching in pockets
for something that's no longer there.

A   It's all pretty simple. And we just complicate it. It's what we're good at.

B   We all write our own histories and we always get them wrong. Writers are probably better at disguising things though. We know that the truth could use some help. And that we're just the ones to do it. What I'm saying is that everyone lies about who they've been and about who they've become. Even to themselves. Mostly to themselves. I have no reason to lie to you. I've probably never met you. Whoever you are I wish you the best. I wish you good things.

We sat there through most of that next day, the evening and the night. He told me most of what I'm telling you now about himself, about his life. Most of these parts about my life I've added later. I told him some of it. I never tell all. Once in a while he'd look up and gaze out the window. Sometime after midnight that second night I saw that when he did this he was looking at his own reflection in the lit glass.

When I was in Grade Five there was a kid in my class, let's call him Walter. His father did a lot of ghost writing. That is not to say that he wrote people's life stories for them so that they could say they wrote it themselves. He stayed up late every night transcribing messages from the dead. Written out in longhand and in pencil on sheets of yellow lined paper. At first it would be gibberish and indecipherable and eventually it would take shape and make sense. He'd sit in the kitchen in the pool of cast light and write for hours. Tearing the finished sheets off the pad as he went and throwing them to the floor. We knew all of this was true because Walter brought in a handful of the sheets to show to us at recess. Only a select few were called out behind the baseball backstop to have a look. We had to admit they looked pretty good. Walter also brought a sample of his father's real handwriting so that we could compare. They were nothing alike. He brought them back one day for show and tell and you could tell Mrs. Watson got very uneasy but we all loved it. We knew somebody whose dad talked to ghosts. It convinced us there was something more.

The writing on the yellow sheets was flowery and delicate. Not like the heavy utilitarian scrawl that had produced a list of measurements on the Bytown Lumber memo pad. What was written on the sheets was by a woman named Eden who said she lived, when she had lived, which was in the late eighteen hundreds, in St. Louis Missourri and had travelled to St. Thomas Ontario with the circus. And she was just one of the many dead people Walter's father was "channelling" which was Walter's word for what his father did. It was pretty amazing. So much so that all that spring a few of us kept getting detentions for coming in late from recess because we were studying new sheets like box scores in the newspaper. St. Thomas was where Jumbo the elephant died. Eden was there when it happened.

We heard later in June that Walter's dad had been sent away for tests and then kept at a special hospital. Apparently he was crazier than wallpaper and none of these voices he'd been writing down were real outside of his own head. Walter didn't bring in any more yellow sheets after that and his dad never showed up for a visit to the class like Walter had promised.

For a while it had been pretty interesting. Everyone, especially the girls, or some of them, really wanted to know what happened to Eden, especially as she had fallen on hard times and it looked as if she was going to end up a prostitute if she didn't stop hanging around the people and places she did. The boys were looking forward to that part. The girls felt certain that they'd missed something. We went back to dodge ball after that. Someone said they saw Walter's dad at the bakery, buying hot cross buns, but that turned out to be Frank, the new guy working at Cavanaugh's Garage, who just looked a bit like Walter's dad. Some of us of course had tried our own hands at spirit writing. It didn't amount to much. Paper was tossed out. Ouija boards put away.

I'm not worried. All of our decay may be forgiven. Will. Then.

A   If you didn't like green
     you could get orange
     and if you didn't like orange
     you could get red
     and if you didn't like red
     you could get black
     those black would take you all the way
     to California
     and back
     in a '53 Chevy
     with no sleep.

     The shining colours.
     What courage
     they seemed. Rumours.

A   I go back to Dyess and it's covered in ghosts. Passing through everything. Waking the living. Look at me. Look at me.

B   Confession: All right. I loved a girl. She stopped loving me back.

     I loved her sister.

     She loved me back. Asked me to stay.

     I left.

Almost married one of them. Maybe had a child with one of them. You'd like to know more about that probably. But this isn't the book. This book is about the big hand of God. How it came down.

There.

A   Confession

    Wrecked every car I ever had
    wrecked other people's too

    indiscriminate.

A   When I left the military I used my GI benefits to sign up for broadcasting school. If no one was going to let me play music I might as well play other people's music. Sam Phillips at Sun Records he told me, "Son, come back when you've done some sinning and give me a record I can sell." I told him that I would. Well, he bought *Folsom Prison* and *Cry, Cry, Cry*. And it was sometime after that and for quite a while after that – I made good on that promise.

B   My mother could see for miles. She was always the first one to see the robin. She saw when you'd done something and you needed to tell her about it. Even when you didn't think you really needed to tell her about it. Even when you thought it might be fine just to keep it to yourself for a little while. She knew better. It was best to come clean.

    Look at this life. All the shining moments. The wreckage. She told me she loved me. I did the same.

    I don't know how many children I have.

Mortality I guess. The concerns of mortality. How the night stretches out from this table forever. When I was young no one spoke of love. It is a physical effort for me, now, to speak of anything else. If you know me you will consider this for a moment and realize it's true. Look around you. All of this is passing. No wonder people start to drink at dusk.

A Don't trust anyone
   I don't
   all of them against me.

   Suddenly know what to do
   a line – invisible,
   from here to there.

A Kristoferson: You're all tangled inside. Have you thought about killing yourself?

   Cash: I know it. You mean today?

B A coil of rope left in the grass. A trail of dead flies by the window. We leave traces of who we believed ourselves to be.

A   There's lots of answers to most questions. Fella came around from *Time Magazine* once and asked me if I thought you had to suffer to play the blues. Well first of all I don't play the blues. Then I think you could make a pretty good case that you have to suffer to play any kind of music. The world likes to think that it loves musicians but it mostly loves them when they're dead.

A   Black Dog

I knew the hound that was chasing me
I knew its determination
its patience.

B   A note on structure:

Ideally three lines is enough to say anything that needs to be said on any topic. But if you'd like to repeat yourself
– you'll need four.

A   A dog barking at night.
I've always known
how it is
when your safe place goes dangerous.

A   People become interviewers for the most part I believe because they've been unsuccessful in finding honest work. How do you feel about this Mr. Cash and what are your views on that Mr. Cash? And they're not interested in the answers. They'll ask me questions about the Native American's treatment by the Government of the United States. They don't give a damn about what this country has done to the Cherokee people. They know I'm likely to say something that's going to sell a few papers. I don't care to sell your papers for you. Seems to me that's your job. Mister, I'm a songwriter and I'm a musician. Find it there.

B   Darkness like a weight – no one allowed in the room and you can't get out from under. It's not something you can do. You simply can't lift yourself up on your own. It can't be done. We lie to ourselves about who we are.

Quiet now.

God reached down into the burned. Wiped the ashes from my eyes. Showed me from how far away he watches. The reporter asked me why I chose such dark themes in my writing. I didn't know how to break it to him. Clearly hadn't heard.

A The way this is now
  I feel almost nothing
  that's a good question I tell the interviewer
  don't even remember what he asked

  my tongue is heavy in my mouth
  I feel like I've been left out to rust
  I feel almost nothing

  where I am is rattling around inside this body
  too tired to care

A I aspire sometimes to feel nothing.

B I seem to pick up feelings from everything around me. It's not
  normal to wonder what the teenaged girl serving you ice cream
  would feel if she were pregnant and had to tell her parents and
  was dreading it with every scoop and every reaching scoop took
  her deeper through the cold into some private corner of her own
  hell. And she just wants to be away somewhere where none of
  this is true anymore. Back before any of this was true. She hasn't
  seen the boy since. He wasn't even from around here, and she
  doesn't want to see him again anyway. She feels numb and
  scared when she even thinks of him. She just feels stupid. That is
  the last thing she wants. And she doesn't know what to do next.
  There's no way past this. Can't see what to do past this next scoop,
  this next order. When she waits for her father to pick her up at the
  end of her shift the moths fly right through the wire cage around

the single yellow light that floods the parking lot. Electricity buzzes in the night and cars pass by slowly, men looking at her. And she is terrified and is at the point now where she can't imagine ever being not terrified again.

Some people can just walk in and buy their damn ice cream cone without shit like this.

I find that I pick up the anxieties of people on television. It's never their joy, their happiness. I've had loaded guns pointed at the base of my skull. I've watched most of my blood drain away into a lake around me. I've opened my eyes in the darkness. I should be able to handle a little Hallmark sad. I should.

I can't watch pain without catching it.

You draw lines in the sand.
I won't cross this one.
I won't cross this one.

In the end you cross them all.

A   Memphis
    Philadelphia
    Dallas
    Detroit
    Toronto
    Halifax
    Paris
    London
    Oslo
    Bergen
    Bourges
    Munich
    Oraz
    Vienna
    Berlin
    Hell

    well
    yes,
    there
    too.

A   God is in the forgiving business, I guess. I never felt he had
    enough reason to forgive me for anything I had done and all the
    things that I hadn't. Found it quite hard to do myself. But I realized
    it was time.

B   Could let so much darkness in. Redemption is a messy business.

A   In 1967, on the southern leg of a North American tour
we stop in at the house where I grew up
they're shooting a documentary
there are these fellows with a camera and microphone
this is in Dyess
and it's all empty
what they called a shotgun shack
because its three rooms lined up one behind the other
and if you fire a shotgun through the front door
it'll shoot on right through the back.
I tell them this
but mostly I keep quiet.
We walk through the rooms – a couch here – a couple of chairs
the shadows of the trees across the walls.
I remember that the day we moved in – 1935
there were five cans of white paint on the floor of the living room
and that was it
everything was white then
or black.

When we first get there
we can't get in.
Someone says "Is it closed up, John?"
I nod yeah
don't say anything
and I move on 'round the back
wander there in the long grass
wander there in the long grass
looking for an opening.

A   "Aren't you Johnny Cash?"

Maybe.

Maybe I am.

B   I like to think that as he's looking into the house, with those dark dog eyes, you can't tell what he's really thinking, but I like to think that he's wondering about the darkness that he's under so much of the time – how it's all an illusion. Except when the lights are out. Except then. I like to think that he's like me and that he's thinking something like that. And I like to think that if he were here now and reading this he'd just nod and we'd share a drink and just sit. One light on in the dark and we'd just sit. But none of this is real. There's only two things in this world I'm afraid of. One of them is me.

A   There's no denying the losses.

A   Over time.

B   This is what he tells me then:

I'm the last one that could be angry with God I really am. It would be ridiculous. There is no cure for autonomic neuropathy, which is apparently what I died from and which was why I could not feel my fingers, my legs, at the end. There is no cure for diabetes. But there is no cure for life either.

I'm not dying. In the hospital I could hear the people in the room rustling around and talking. And I wanted to wake up and tell them. *I'm not dying.*

I'm not.

A   I can't walk past a church if there's music playing. I remember one particularly hard morning in Memphis and a sky full of teeth bearing down on me. It was cold like only a March morning can be cold and if it hadn't been for the First Baptist Church and the choir bleeding out into the street and the girl taking the lead and her voice sounding like there was a light coming out of it… and there was. If it hadn't been for that and so many other things now that I see were pointing me along the way. I've always felt most comfortable around people who know where they're going. Where they're bound. I've felt privileged to be around them and for a time to call myself one.

A   What I did about love

jumped up, ran at full speed
and put my fist through the wall

at that moment
it was all I could do.

Did it.

Then outside with only a towel on. The blood snaking down my arm. Salt.

B   My demons

    and this life,
    so strange and unyielding

    running is the thing
    really running
    put on that extra burst of speed I mean

    but they're fast

    they're so fast.

    Don't tell me you've got the blues. Don't say that you know what it is to have demons. If you haven't seen death as preferable to what you're feeling – then you don't know.

A   Ladies and Gentlemen Miss June Carter.

"Well Cash?" she'd say.

Way she lit up and her already burning so bright. I ran on that fuel for years. Still running.

Sometimes I like just to watch her hands on the autoharp
her hands like those of so many good women before her
and she the best of them.

She picked me up
like it was nothing
just to save a man
from himself.

One foot there
catches in the light
poking out from the sheets
turning.

I know she's tired,
I'm tired too.

A   I'm not the man I was before. And that's the story there. I'm never the man I think I am.

B There's an evening in late July when the sun is just down at the edges of the cornrows south of town and you're driving a big car with the top down. You realize all that darkness might be gone. It doesn't have to be a good car, you understand, just a big one. Robert Johnson would have wanted it to be a big car. J.R. would have made sure it was.

A   June's like one of those little wood stoves
    they have in the hunting camps up north
    I think they call them Quebec heaters
    getting into bed
    it's like getting into bed with
    new fired bricks

    so I'm never cold
    anymore.

A   it was like crows shot out of the air
    every word that I said to her
    falling
    till the floor was covered
    the room full of everything I'd never done
    for her.

B   When you're almost killed a number of times it lends a certain perspective. When it happens eight times, well, it lends a sense of peace. And urgency too. I drove out this evening to the NAPA store and bought a new shift knob for the Jeep. It's an eight ball. If I some day have a son I'll pass it on to him. And I'd tell him why. It would be important for him to know why.

    He could keep the eight ball. Put it away in a box in his closet. Someday put it in a car of his own. I don't have much of value to pass on. There's an old Rolex that doesn't work anymore. There's the Jeep, I own that outright now. There are these stories of mine. There's the eight ball, shining and black. What a thing to give.

A   This spring feeds the pond
      the one I made
      and stocked with fish.
      I like to sit by the side.
      Each year
      I plant a new tree –
      pine
      weeping willow
      pin oak
      willow oak
      magnolia
      cedar –
      solid trees
      pretty trees

      no shirt
      no shoes.

      Way she leaves a room
      same way she comes in
      like she knows where she's going.

      I'm more tentative,
      never know
      what's around the corner.

A   Luther Perkins played a Fender Telecaster with the heel plate missing
      and he'd lay his right hand over the strings
      to mute them when he played
      that's where the boom-chicka-boom sound came from

and that's the sound playing when I walked out
this is 1968 Folsom Prison
you have to understand
this is either a comeback
or the end
and this is not an easy crowd.
These are hard men
any one of them could shiv you as easy as clap for you
but man they clap
like it's for some kind of a saviour
you can hear it on the tapes
and I'm walking right out there
with a black suit and a guitar.

B   There are two men here,
one wants to kill me
and the other wants to save me
and one of them has to die.

I can hear the trucks out on the highway.
How long have the three of us been
sitting here?

A   These vines
      come from cuttings from Hendersonville
      and those in turn
      from my parent's house
      carried to Tennessee
      wrapped in wet newspaper
      inside a suitcase
      dark pools of water stain the lining.
      Early to mid May
      with the first of the hot days here
      you cut off five joints of second-year growth,
      two joints down and two above,
      you work them in like this
      and cover them over nicely
      like this
      manure and water
      and watch them go.
      They'll produce more than I can use I know
      but that's the way He is
      when He's not batting you around
      He's just waiting on you
      gracious.

A   It was just after I bought the Cadillac and I was driving Roseanne to riding lessons. Funny enough the way I grew up and who I am, the first time I learned to ride was on a movie set. In the field coming up on my side I could see a young girl and a pony in the morning grass and I said Roseanne look at the pony honey and she said wait daddy I have to get my seatbelt on and I said but just look for a minute because I knew she loved to see horses and

I knew we'd be past it by the time she was done and she looked up at me and said daddy death won't wait for a pony

and I just looked back at her and I said no honey I guess that's so and I just kept my eyes on the road after that because I was thinking of course of Jack.

B   These nights when I can't sleep I just take down the Bible and I read. I believe it makes me a better person. Not better than anyone else, you understand. Better than myself.

A   Hickory Lake:
    home from a tour – winter comes
    Please mister god
    big mister God
    I'll hold out
    but you know that I will let you down
    again.
    Stay with me.

    There are still places I have
    never seen
    and certain movements of my heart
    which made glad my young days.

    I don't know.
    You make the choices you make
    and that's that.

    The air this morning is full of wings
    and the first Tennessee snow has fallen,
    already the lake is beginning to ice
    and the air is hard and close.

    Abide.

    I reach out my hands
    to this world

    and I am
    astonished.

A   Hickory Lake: everything is fragile – spring comes

There is a frailty
in all our music.

It is warmer today
and the sun wets the tops of the frozen trees
shining them
for the moment they are new
the wood cracks
the dog turns, chases something in the field
turns again
tests the air
barks
he's unsure
water drops steady and bright from the branches
bronze and rose
the wet wood –

this life burns so pretty –

I watch John Carter
running out to meet the dog,
the size and breadth of his life
reaching out
to fill him up.

All the time in the world

and I whisper fast

spare him too.

B   Confession

    I don't drink any longer

    no pills

    I pray

    sometimes with such force

    I swoon

    I sway

    and the next day

    my head hurts

    as if emptied

    filled

    and then emptied once more.

A   There's a storm coming
       electric down the highway
       the vaulting sky over the tour bus.

       I get up early
       and I pray
       for about twenty minutes
       for the world, for June and the children and the grandchildren,
       mostly for myself
       I need all the help I can get

       and I've stopped drinking
       and pills
       really stopped this time
       so that's about it then

       lightning now
       a shining presence behind everything

       and I'm coming home
       and I'm
       glad at heart.

A   Once a woman appeared
       in our dining room –
       there were six of us there –

       and we all saw the same.
       She came through the door

leading to the kitchen
in a full-length white dress

proceeded across the room
went through the double doors
without opening them first

and then knocked
from the other side
rat-a-tat,
rat-a-tat

but there's things more dangerous
in this world
than all the dead
put together.

B   "Do you mind if I ask you something?"

His voice has changed and he's eyeing me a little more carefully.
He's sizing me up, feels like. Taking the measure.

"Go ahead," I say.

Cash moves the bottle to one side of the table so there's nothing
between us now but two shot glasses, his empty.

"What the hell are you doing here?"

For a moment I look around the little kitchen. The bare wood walls and plank floor. He bolts up suddenly like a jack-knifed field snake, the table flipping and his big hands are on my throat like he's caught a rabbit and means to kill the life right out of it. I grab onto his arms and try to pry them off as the table flips over and we end up on the floor, bottle spinning, Cash's knee up on my chest, his hands still at my throat and me gasping for air. I'm trying to turn away to the right and left at the same time, trying to get my legs going. Cash's face is tight over me, in a corkscrew smile.

"I mean... what the fuck... are you... still doing here?"

And I don't know if he means in this house or in this life. And I can't answer anyway. My lungs are screaming. I don't know. I don't know.

A   I liked the back roads and alleys best
    liked to ride the rails
    because they always took you into the ass end of a town first
    the part the mayor and town council didn't want you to see
    that way when they gave you the key to the city
    you knew what you were really getting

A   Reach and pick a drowning moth from the whisky
    nothing deserves to die that way though
    many do

B   One thing you could always say about Johnny
    he was true
    even there with his knee deep into my chest
    he was gospel.

A   After the concert some lady asked,
    John are you truly a believer?
    and I said
    Ma'am with a list of sins this long
    how could I not be?

    Maybe it seemed flippant
    but I meant it.

A   A Legion of Whispers

    After the fight we had
    I end up on this bench
    looking down at my upturned hands.

    Those things we said
    to each other
    things we yelled at each other,

    I'm sorry, June
    what I meant to say was I love you
    but that's not the way
    it came out

    and I think of God
    who carries
    us all

    and I say a good prayer
    to the good night

    feel the flow of blood in my body
    see the slant of silver light.

    I will learn from that woman walking,
    from the way that branch
    lifts in the wind.
    I can learn from anything.

B   I have no regrets
    I carry no guilt

    bear no ill will

    there are reductions in everything of course.

    But not everything dies. Not everything leaves.

A   Steel is hard because it knew the hammer
       and that's what love does
       turns a bad man good
       and a good man better
       and of course it can tear at you too
       down to nothing
       we were lucky

A   The man comes around

       June I want more than anything
       to know that you are
       happy now

       I want that
       more than anything

B   I've been thinking
       I think that I am a good man
       I don't think
       that's going to be enough

A No longer a young man
  these lines track
  the trouble I've seen
  these tears

  the losses I've taken
  keep me humble
  prevent the wearing
  of any crowns

A Absolution

  I stood backstage in Fredericton that night a little longer than usual
  but I always stood alone
  before going onto stage

  if I met people afterwards
  and I felt as if I should do that
  I was always uncomfortable

  met that poet with the unusual name
  then the prince of England –
  how strange this path is.

B he was not a man
  for the entourage
  he often preferred to be alone

when he finally let me up off the floor
set me up and brushed my shoulders
he looked abashed

as if I'd forced him to reveal the secret of a magic trick
or caught him cheating
cards up his sleeve

"I should be on my way"
he said
"I'm keeping you from your work..."

and I wanted to tell him
Stay as long as you like
I poured us another drink

and we sat in silence

and the next morning he was gone

ALDEN

HOLLOW-BONED BLUES

A   the baby is still crying, this bread has mould
      the baby is still crying and this bread has mould
      children can exist in worlds adults would die to leave

A   When I was a little boy
      I had no idea that poverty
      was a condition
      from which I suffered
      I'd pick flowers for my mother
      come running home with them
      once I became convinced
      that God was going to kill everyone
      by dropping clouds
      on their heads.

      The events of my life
      were going to happen to me.
      I would have been shocked.
      A dish of salt. Hard wide plank floor. A small voice singing.

B   At the University of Calgary
      there's a stockpile of Nowlan papers
      newspaper articles
      diary entries
      clippings
      original manuscripts
      just about anything
      and really

I should go
just pack up the Jeep
and drive out there.
A Canadian poetry adventure!
But I won't. Should go somewhere though.
Should go somewhere.
Go.

A   In other parts of the continent my people would have been called
    crackers
    rednecks
    straw hatters
    peckerwoods

    the spiritual survivors
    of legendary lost colonies
    frontiersmen
    in an era when there is no longer
    a geographical frontier.

A   Four Bars

    When I was five
    my father read to me from a book
    kept up on a shelf
    I'd sit quietly and listen
    rapt
    and when my father left
    to chase through the bars
    I begged my mother to read
    and she took the book down and began.
    Dull.
    Well I threw myself to the floor
    it wasn't the same story
    my father who couldn't read
    had been making it all
    up.

Well I threw myself to the floor
I threw myself
this was before the Governor General's gardens
the kind words.

B   Alden describes hitching thirty kilometres into town to buy old books and the sensuous feel of them against his chest on the trudge home, like the feel of a sleeping young girl's head against a young boy's shoulder. I remember leafing through books and smelling deeply along their open spines. I remember doing this before I was old enough to draw any appropriate analogies.

I believed that the books would take me somewhere. And they did. They have brought me here.

A   When I was young
life in this country
was a grim affair
everything was in black and white

news came second-hand
it was difficult to find what you really wanted
at Freemans
or the Hudson Bay Company

the only official language
was small
and no one really understood it
though they pretended to.

Men could choose to go to work
in trim grey suits
or they could fish, or cut wood
that was it.

Women had few choices
other than to marry the men
but we had Don Messer
the Toronto Maple Leafs

and biere froide
it wasn't so bad
you could smoke as many cigarettes as you wanted
and nobody had yet figured out

that we were mortal.

A   Confession

    My father then
    I'm the only one
    who ever feared him.

B   There are books to be had nearby though and I love
    you know
    sifting through them
    you run across photos

    Alden Nowlan in Ireland
    in one of them.

    Alden Nowlan in Cuba
    in another.

    Only it's the same picture
    which is delightful really
    in what it might say about the man himself
    this lack of pinning down.

    There are five people in the picture
    but only one of them
    is claiming to be Alden Nowlan.

    Sitting on the back of a park bench
    fallen socks, a smile.

A   I realized later in life
that my father's poverty
had nothing to do
with money.

A   My father's wisdom:

not for nothin'
but if I was to hold your head under water for ten minutes
I guess you'd come up dead
or not come up at all…

apropos of nothing,
just warning
or observation,
maybe just advice.

B   It's something I should do
certainly

this packing of the Jeep
this driving off to Nova Scotia
to see the house

this is poetry after all
so there is no budget and
you can just pretend

but I do it anyway.

Go

Johnny said

I went.

Nothing keeping me fixed to place

hard   beautiful   open

road

A   Folks around Stanley liked my father mostly
    but it was because of his sad antics
    it was because on his benders he didn't hurt anyone
    or burn anything down

    it wasn't liking really
    more like a gratitude
    it was like a tolerance
    they could afford.

A   My father speaks:

    talk is cheap

    he says

    but it takes money to buy rum.

B   It is now early morning, was a bad night. The motel room seems
    large. The morning sun has concentrated all the cigarette smoke
    so you can see it hanging in pillars or sliding along the ceiling
    like amoebae. In the bathroom, I wash the loose nicotine out of my
    mouth. I smell the smoke still in my shirt. Swallow fire.

    I've driven two days solid and I've found this motel near Alden's
    childhood. It shoulders the road like he shouldered his life. It is a
    favourite of bikers passing through to Quebec. The curtains are
    the colour of tobacco. I'm not alone.

A   Their search for happiness led them here
    where my father eventually kicked my mother from the house
    for stepping out with younger men
    she took us to live with my uncle and aunt
    and I'd spend Sunday afternoons
    in the outhouse with Uncle Albert
    the door open
    my uncle taking pot shots with his .45 at the clothespins on the line
    until my outraged mother
    would chase us both with a broom

    she would sit up herself
    late into the moonless nights
    with a .22 across her lap
    occasionally rousing the whole house
    with a shot

    nobody knew what at.

A   *Grace is away*
    she wrote me she might possibly be up Sunday
    but I don't know
    Alden is home now
    with the father
    Alden was down to see me
    three or four times
    all by himself
    such a big boy he is getting to be
    he will start school this fall too

*I hope he likes to go
and goes every day*

I just don't know about him

B   The sound of the tap has woken her. Only her left foot turns out from the bottom of the sheets when she starts to move. There's the sound of the trucks now on the highway. It has started to rain. The window vibrates.

A   *that family*
    when his mother was took up with Collins
    and hadn't seen her own kids in weeks
    she'd pass by her own son
    in Collins' old car
    sitting there in the passenger seat
    grand as you please
    and give no sign
    to her own son
    not a wave
    imagine
    how that must feel to the boy

    her own son
    left standing there
    all torn down inside

A   Arch Campbell
    lit up enough to ride his horse through Stanley at a full gallop
    on a moonless night
    and certain enough hit a hole
    and got tangled up
    and died on the ground
    of a broken neck
    and still holding the reins

    Billy Freeman
    who had one arm shorter than the other
    but still worked the mill
    and spent most everything he earned on Saturday night

folks called him The Clock
one arm shorter than the other don't you see.

Davis MacSkimming
lit up just about every night
people called him The Moth
because he'd stop at every light
on the way home.

At this point the fiddle music starts –
it's soft and it's beautiful –
and it covers up some of the pain
of devastated lives
like these.

B   She wants me to wash her hair. She wants a cigarette. I want to tell her that I'm looking for the childhood home of the great Canadian poet Alden Nowlan. I want to tell her that I'm in the middle of something. I tell her that this combination of black hair and grey eyes is deeply unsettling. She was standing next to the rack of plastic lobsters at the Irving stop at two in the morning. Skin beautiful even in the fluorescent light. I want to tell her that she has probably made a bad choice of companion. I want to tell her that maybe I have done the same. I start the bath. Blue and green dove flying at her ankle. Maybe. Maybe Cash was right. I could tell her the truth. Could. It's not too late and in a moment.

A   Stanley NS, 1945

　　We watched the end of the driveway
　　as a flock of crows
　　shadowed overhead
　　the tired grass burning in the sun
　　as Mrs. Edwards across the street pulled back her drapes
　　and stood watching too.

　　The heat was unbearable
　　softening the pavement
　　heating the rubber of the one tire of Jimmy Edward's bicycle
　　that turned in the air,
　　the other so badly mangled
　　by the impact of the car fender
　　that it looked unlikely to ever turn again.
　　We watched
　　as the car door slammed and the man ran back
　　swearing.

　　None of us knew then that Japan had surrendered.

　　Mrs. Edward's mouth open
　　her too-white hand silently pushing the glass.

A   The Local Scene

　　Look, I'll tell you this
　　but don't get it wrong

people get so many things wrong
and they haven't been where I have.

This fellow
I don't even remember his name
he's always swearing
Cuss Cannon, we called him
he thinks we should lay in wait
in behind the mill
for this girl to come walking home from school
and we do
and we're talking about raping her
talking about it
and she never shows that day
I find out later he's a psychotic

and we never go back.

B   When I finish drying her hair she rests a new cigarette on the side of the sink and asks me what it is that I need saving from. I dry my hands. A long vodka trail last night. Maybe she thinks it's her.

But it's so obviously me that I have to look away.

A   Consider the kid in the picture
     twelve
     snot nosed
     ill-fed

     picked up the pen
     started to

     of all god forsaken things

     write it down
     barren on the page.

A   The typewriter arrived finally by eastbound
     ordered from the Eaton's catalogue
     there was no place in Stanley to buy one
     and it took most of the tree cutting pay
     but I knew that being a writer
     required it
     it arrived without any manual
     spent several days
     learning all of the different keys

     and there was a girl

     I loved
     afraid to
     say.

B   *Alden is not specific about it.*

I tell her at the restaurant which is attached to the glass walled
lobby of the motel in a 1970's dream of convenience.

Being in the madhouse:
sometimes he calls it that
and himself a *patient*
sometimes he's a *visitor*
because his *uncle* worked there
sometimes it's he himself who worked there
and that's not *true*, there are no records of him as an employee.

She's wearing large white-framed sunglasses
a small grey sweater.
The rain has stopped.

His mother trained there briefly
and she claims to have *been* there
when he was a patient
and been turned away
by her own son.
This is in 1946
and Alden would have been thirteen
admitted to the Nova Scotia Hospital in Halifax
because his chest was "stove in" –

she winces
her name is Heather –

and he was pale
and wouldn't eat

plus he'd constructed a stone church
in the backyard
and could be *heard* in there late at night
howling damnation and visions
so it wasn't just his *appetite*.
Grace probably *made up* the story about being turned away
It is known that Alden was taught to play baseball while he was there
and given books
but his main problem
as his aunt stated it
was that *he thought no one loved him*.
Across the highway from the motel there's a park with picnic tables
the clouds break and the sun passes quickly over the grass.

But let's be clear about it
I tell her
no one did.

And then a man the colour, shape and dimensions of Alden Nowlan walks into the restaurant, pauses as the aluminum door swings closed behind him, squints through coke bottle glasses at the menu overhead and orders two crullers and a large coffee. Sits down at the counter next to us and looks at me. I refuse to be surprised.

Heather introduces herself and begins to discuss her doctoral dissertation which she has "so far anyway" titled *The Poetics of Place: East Coast Poetry 1930 to1950*. I realize that she is the type of person who can talk to anybody.

"My father never learned to drive a car..." Alden says.

When you're splitting wood the gravity does most of the work. When you write you're on your own. A little boy alone in a car in the parking lot is playing the radio too loud. His mother yells at him from the open door of their motel room. She waves her arms in a downward motion. Heather laughs at something Alden has said. A chambermaid turns out of a room with an armload of blankets. There's a grey sky rolling across the highway and the wind has picked up. The boy turns the music down. Heather has taken off her sunglasses. The little lines at the corners of her eyes. I am

unhinged.

A   In Stanley
the sun seemed to drop right through the ground
as if yanked by magnets

(like it had no interest in staying around)

A   We all come quite slowly to realize the things that we are good at. It's an ongoing process of elimination. I once thought that I'd try my hand at the fiddle. If Don Messer could do it, then why not me? Apparently there were many reasons.

I picked up an old fiddle at a pawn shop and I hammered away at it for a while. Sawed, I suppose, would be more accurate.

I thought that I wasn't too bad and I thought that with a few lessons, well, maybe I could do no harm in playing a few tunes for a few people. Wiser heads prevailed. Mrs. Linklater, who had been selected for the task of elevating my rough-hewn talent into something more presentable, watched from a safe distance in the corner of her parlour for a time while the performing bear in the corduroy jacket lumbered about the room elbowing away and disturbing the furniture. She kept one hand in the pocket of her crocheted sweater and one to her mouth. It was the sort of expression one might see in the countenance of someone witnessing a tragic automobile accident. Eventually she reached out and forcibly removed the instrument from my hands. "Give me that before you hurt someone with it!" and then she set it down carefully on the little table near the centre of the room.

"That amount of playing should serve well for a first lesson," she said softly, touching the fret of the instrument in a thoughtful manner. Some, she told me, are born to play the fiddle and some to be of service to the community in other ways, such as leading a Boy Scout troup or joining the Rotary Club.

She was quite delicate about it all and offered me a cup of tea before I left.

The way she touched the instrument with reverence.

B   I have this
recurring nightmare that I am thirty again
and realize
it's too late.

I wake up
I write to fix things that are broken
it's not
too late yet.

It is not my wish to try for redemption through a woman. Not again. Heather's body is a tool for opening me up though. Her slow gaze carefully rearranging.

A woman came after me once with a knife. Her trembling hands. Blood gone from her face like poplar leaves turned in the wind. A storm is coming certain and low now over the motel. The first big cold drops hit. Heather has come back. She turns the arm of her sunglasses against her teeth. Smiles, for what I think is no reason.

A   Alden says:

    I can laugh.
    I do laugh.
    I shall die of laughter.

A   Because Harriet needed to marry him I suppose
    or to escape

    I took up a pen
    and forged our father's name
    on the paper that gave his consent
    her the future she thought she wanted
    while her boyfriend
    waited in the car.

    That same year I wrote several things
    on a resume
    that had never actually happened –
    finishing school
    even high school
    and a job with a newspaper!
    These things could have happened
    I suppose
    but easier just to say they did,
    write them into being
    so much, indeed, for the sword!

B   When he left

He took with him
a small cardboard suitcase
some books.

The Telegraph-Journal
printed an article
a year after his death
about the house in Stanley
a family lived there now
and had found
in a pasture
an old rusted typewriter
the long grass
crowding its keys

like many other things
too difficult
for him
to carry.

This pencil now
focussing me down.

The way she hums her thoughts
looks away
that roped hair across her skin in the dark
soft as grace
the way the skin just below her navel or the small of her back
is softer than any word I can think of
to describe.

A   What would I have been?

      left behind the mill
      left behind the house
      left behind the family
      and everyone I knew

      I rode up through snow, up and out of the life I was living.

A   How could you know?

      this is it you see
      the reason and the why
      the what and the if
      the rise and inevitable
      the talon and the crumb
      the alpha and the rest of it
      the Grand Guignol of it
      the restless coming to
      the thousand miles gone
      the duct tape on the window
      the tired fridge
      the relentless surprise
      the heart loose in the throat
      the ice in the wind
      the house next door
      burnt down to the ground
      black frame naked

the white ankles

the this and the what comes after

the long thin line of the

B   Late into the afternoon and more drunk than you have a right to be for the time of day and wondering now how you'll possibly survive the night at this rate. And then you stop worrying and let the swirl of discussion take you again. The storm clattering at the window.

And later – her question about love:

what are you doing?
whatever you'll let me

A   In Hartland
     there was a brief period
     when I was thin and respectable,
     women pointed me out to their daughters
     as an eligible catch
     and the wives
     of most of my bourgeois friends
     were willing to sleep with me
     because I was younger
     than their husbands
     and very,
     very discreet.

A   The problem now with going to bed in Hartland
     is that when you wake up
     you're still in Hartland, the dark has removed nothing
     the rail cars still in the yard covered in grey wet

     so you hover over the eggs
     you hover over the eggs
     what else is there for you to do?
     No pretty here, no respite

     the CBC plays the only interview Willie Johnson ever gave
     he says people think there's a train to heaven
     and a train to hell
     says "there ain't but one train and you're either on it, or you're not"

     and I write that down the pencil grooving through the paper and
     into the soft wood of the table
     write something about hollowed eyes and eyes burnt by the sun
     rain now slicing against the glass

but I'm not afraid
anymore. I'm not.

B   Only we were both suddenly somebody else

This window is stuck
beyond it the trucks glide by
the storm has passed
I'm tired suddenly with this struggle
even with making love
tired now of the window
and of everything else.
The grey afternoon stretches out in all directions
our lives
behind this window
all lit up
with the dark.
It's almost five o'clock now
the television drones a game show
the weak light reflected in the glass
Alden gone.

The moon rises pale
and the shivering trucks
continue by
fewer of them
but I have a friend
I do
and she turns against me in the sheets.

A   Claudine shaking –
      calling me to the driveway in the pouring rain
      the blood fur matted fender
      she's killed a deer.
      I tell her it's probably okay,
      probably still running,
      a cup of tea and to bed.
      my clothes still damp on the hanger,
      leaving the light on,
      not knowing why.

A   Uncertain then certain

      I escaped to New Brunswick
      to start a job at the *Observer*.
      Within a week I was sorting through boxes in the office basement
      with John Diefenbaker who was visiting.
      In a dank room with years of clippings
      Santa Claus notes, church revivals...
      Dief was looking for the text
      of a speech
      that had been reprinted in the paper.
      We found it easily enough
      and Dief read through it
      at the end of every sentence he stopped
      and gave a satisfied grunt
      as if to say
      I was right there

or
*that was a fine point
I made.*

I didn't mind
I was a little star-struck

In Hartland women stopped me on the street
to say hello!
I knew they were checking on me
they'd heard I was strange
but it was all right
I was!
No one had ever bothered back in Stanley
to verify it
they'd never have taken the time –

little hats and flower print dresses
and always so sweet.

B   There's nothing like the head you get at three o'clock in the morning
when you start to drink in the afternoon and you don't let up
and then fall asleep early.

She wakes up with me and holds the sheet to herself while I drink
water from the scuffed bathroom glass.

I tell her about the house I grew up in
the paper Santa Claus on the door each Christmas
how it's run down now, the concrete steps slowly sinking into the
ground

and she says isn't it a shame
we're all going to die

and isn't it beautiful

we're   *all*   going to die.

A   And I stand regarding my father's house, which is not there

It was modest by anyone's standards
but serviceable
gradually whittled away
first the second floor shut off
after Grace and us kids took off
because it was too hard to heat
from the woodstove in the kitchen.

My father's remaining ambitions
died off
so too did the two goats and the sheep
eaten
or sold
the machinery rusted
lilac and rose overtook the lawn
eventually he was down to a cot in the kitchen
too tired
to keep the other rooms open
nobody in them anyway

I remember
eating pepper sandwiches
as a boy
the bread blackened.

Slap sandwiches
you'd slap the butter on
and slap the bread together
because there was nothing else.

The way that some women know to undo us, to make us tell them
what we didn't know until they asked us.

children found my father's body
there was no one so alone as he.

A   Certain he was a hammer swinger
but he never had anything to hit.
All gravy,
no bread.
The way a photograph can tell you something you knew but
didn't.

B   One thing Alden is doing
throughout
I think
whether he knows it or not

hoping that God is listening.

We take the canvas off the Jeep for the drive back to the motel with
liquor and sandwiches.
He sits expansively in the little rear seat
his corduroy knees pressed against our backs
laughing suddenly,
all of us,
at something we can't name.

A When I think about
  the things that I can –
  pulling apples from a tree
  climbing
  with a little girl named Katherine
  her white socks.

  There used to be wild deer across the river
  one of them wore a bell
  and no one knew why
  that story long lost.

  I pull these things from the air
  small details
  like lights.

A When I Hear the Dead Singing

  Abandoned by my mother
  beaten by my father

  I could write that.

  Why would I write that?

  I could write that.
  I do.

  When my father died there were his tools to deal with
  no one knew
  what to do with these.

B   You create that upon which your attention is focused.

Funny thing about Cash was that he was immaculate. I think about that, now, getting dressed. Not that you wouldn't expect him to be but he was overly immaculate. I once saw one of Elvis's jumpsuits in person and it was far less turned out than you'd imagine. It was sweat-lined and brown-collared. Shabby under museum lights. Much smaller too than you'd think.

Cash wasn't like that. His cuffs were permanently shot from the sleeves of his jacket. Even when we'd been struggling over the kitchen table, chairs tipping back and shot glasses falling, his hair was brilliantined perfectly, his collar sharp. In death he was the stage but the hands that gripped my throat and eventually worked me down to the floor, those were all J.R. As the air was being choked out of me, his knee on my chest, I remember thinking

"Larger than life… hell yes."

Saltier language too, at that moment, than you'd expect from a vision. His shoes were like black mirrors, but you knew they could deliver a first-class shit-kicking.

I checked the mirror again. Had to look good. Tried to adopt some of J.R.'s swagger. No, she'd see right through that.

A   Once I was out flying a kite, Alden says

    with my girlfriend's little boy
    doesn't that sound ridiculous:
    my girlfriend's little boy.
    Great fun.
    I didn't give a damn
    about being a writer
    or anything else, nothing
    except getting that kite higher up
    than Johnnie had ever seen a kite go before.

    The heart
    its secret embarkations

A   universal love song

    I grovelled
    before the local Bank Manager
    crawled in on my hands and knees
    licking the dust at his feet
    except there ain't any dust
    in banks

    "I believe in people anyway, not banks."

    "To people, I say."

B   The waiter balances menus
      Heather balances her coffee

      Look, I tell her, I'm in love with you
      I'm telling you that

      now

      your small hands
      I say.

      Then later
      "You've got me where you want me." she says. "Now."
      Light left on. Bugs against the screen.
      Sudden blood from her bitten lip.
      Metal taste wiped away.

A   Might not change a lot maybe nothing at all
    given the chance
    I have Claudine and Johnnie of course
    there's a chair in the living room I've become quite fond of
    I enjoy ham sandwiches
    the sound of the percolator
    darkness bubbling in the little glass dome.
    With a blanket for my knees on a wet morning in the fall
    I'll watch the leaves from the bay window
    tracking their way up Davis Street
    heedless
    and I don't care you see
    I've beaten them all
    or enough of them to announce myself king
    with this crown I've fashioned from yesterday's Gleaner
    the tin foil wrapper from the frozen fish

    and His Majesty decrees no tears today

    the black and the white the truth and the rest of it.

A   sunshine
    sunshine sunshine sunshine and lollipops
    lost loves and barrooms

    where are the songs of the lost warrior monarchs
    valiant leaders
    what have we done with all our heroes?

B   always convinced I would die in a car crash
then had one and switched it over to cancer
but that seemed presumptuous

I'm now fairly certain, having been threatened with guns and knives
that it will be a pearl onion that will take me down or an olive
my face turning blue on the carpet vodka or gin soaking the wood
at any rate I'm ready.

A   Love, I guess, is the way that you'd put it
    the way that it is
    Claudine was more important to me
    than I was
    am.

A   Quote

    If there comes a time
    when truck drivers read poetry

    mine will be the poetry
    they read.

B   The way to put it
    when I watch her these mornings
    naked around the room
    she has this way of moving
    as if denying
    that her presence is a benediction
    the measure of her
    in every small gesture.

A   Claudine loved me
can you imagine that?
and she knew me!

knew everything I had
and hadn't done

A   The Water at Morning

This is what I wanted you to know, Claudine
that I stood at the window in my bathrobe
and watched the fishing boats head out of the harbour
fighting the chop

that I wished them well.

Wished them a full catch
and back with their hulls bursting.
Wished you were there with me
to see the way the water fights them
but holds them up too.
There's a button off my red shirt
I miss you.

B   We sit looking out over the little harbour. I tell her about the girl who came after me with a knife. And how I grabbed it by the blade. Waited for my fingers to fall. And then how she ran into the road and in front of a truck. How I pulled her out at the last second and felt the displaced air brush against my leg. The look she'd had on her face waiting for the impact. That look. I tell her things that are true. Things I've done. I tell her I have a trick to show her and I put my hands out.

"Push against them," I say, "hard as you can…"

She does and I push back.

"I've heard about this" she says, her body tensed.

"Now loosen up," I say, "Let them go…"

And I take her small hands in mine and shake them gently, and then ball them together.

"C'mon, let me have them…"

And she does and I quickly bring them to my mouth and kiss them.

"I told you it was a trick."

Her smooth skin.

There's a small boat just cresting the waves and there's a sun break in the clouds. I tell her things that are true. Because I can. There's no reason

to make things up.

A   Pale light, cloudless sky

       and Claudine would have been happier
       I know
       if I were something more straightforward
       and working class,
       a truck driver, for instance
       one who went to the pub
       on Saturday nights
       with the other truck drivers
       while she and the other truck drivers' wives
       went off to play bingo
       I sound as if I'm complaining.
       but I'm not
       at least I don't think I am.

       I've learned to adapt to prosperity.

A   Do. Make. Say. Think. Sleep. Talk. Eat. Wash. Drink. Talk some more. So many things to do that it's a wonder anything ever gets done. So many things that it's like a carnival. I stand outside after supper and have a smoke. There's a fella down the road still hasn't taken his plastic Santa face out of the window and it's June. The window shows south and the face is sun-bleached a pure white – an albino Santa. Come to think of it I believe it was there all last year too. He's got no problems with productivity and the passage of time.

My heart, my heart. Maybe lasting. Maybe calm.

B   The way she steals a kiss. Reaching up. Taking it. A quick breath.

A One Sunday afternoon Johnnie was playing down the cellar. It was all right. He was all right down there on his own. He had that record playing again. Setting up his army men. Knocking them down. It was tough to get a poem going with that music on. Our lives before us

 pulling us on.

A 1983 League of Canadian Poets Western Tour

 Somehow I give the wrong directions to the driver
 we end up at the wrong end of the campus
 and I clamber up on some boxes
 peer into empty classrooms

 and after at the pub I win a draft beer drinking contest!

B There's a dog limping out by the cars under the fluorescent lights. Strange time and place for a dog. It'll be okay. The world so loves a flawed hero.

A   Layton: How is it that you poets from the Maritimes are all such big men?

Nowlan: All our little poets are beaten to death before the age of twelve.

A   What I'm asking about is feeling like you're being torn apart by good and evil every day. Don't you ever feel that way? If I'd got up the nerve I was going to ask Cash about that, if I'd got the chance and got up the nerve as I say. At least I had hoped that I wouldn't just pony up with, Well I really enjoy your music or some such slop. And then the goddamned Prince of Wales walks in. Oh well.

I know lots of poets who don't believe in God but I don't know of any Gods who don't believe in poets. And our God, the God, sometimes I think we just made him up to avoid the responsibility of who we are. But to leave the world having done more good than harm – that would be splendid now.

B   I've been to the places the devil would want me to be. I know where the crossroads are. Felt the dust between my toes.

I once held a man underwater, just to watch his face turn.

I have seen the face of evil. It's not hot and flaming. It's calm.

It's cold. And it knows such rejoicing.

A   I met June Carter Cash
       and I told her
       right out
      "Miss Carter I have long been of the opinion that you have the sexiest right knee in show business."

      She replied "Thank you very much, Sir, for noticing."

      Imagine that:

      Sir

A   Cash tore up the songs he sang that night
       like a manic preacher
       like someone who'd been to the mountaintop
       and been kicked down the other side of it

      I'd seen worse addicts
      never a better entertainer.

B   Someone will find. That dog.

A   The world
    in its fashion
    has been kind
    overall

    The doctor said I had cancer
    his voice fuzzy and indistinct
    said my chances the same
    as those of a Canadian soldier landing at Dieppe in '42

    and I was laughing –
    what else are we to do? –
    I went in for a sore throat.

A   Cheerless Surroundings

    Sometimes I get so damned lonely, and drunk always drunk too, that I pick up the phone and call night operators all over Canada and the United States. I know a girl in Texas who wants to make me a cherry cobbler! Wonderful that I should know so many women without ever laying an eye (or a hand!) on any of them. This is called roostering for skirts but usually it's done in a dance hall or saloon. Leave it to me to do the job by long distance.

    I'm not sure why I get so damned lonely. No one around of course that does it but it's something else too. Something deep inside that calls out when there's nothing there.

    It takes an effort for me to be happy. I have to keep reminding myself.

Take my advice – look hard into your soul – things go quicker than you think.

B   Indeed. See. What did I tell you?

A   they find these little gowns to put you in
as if the sickness on you wasn't enough
they single you out.

A   What I would choose if I were choosing would not be this. Neck tied in these damn bandages and a regular fire going on in there. Why the hell would anyone think to paint the walls of a hospital room grey? Enough grey in the world already. Light grey wall slightly darker shining grey metal window edge grey steel sky sinking down greyer wall of building. Bandages keeping the heat in. Damn damn and damn and well…could drink a well dry. And too many drugs by a damned sight. Too many bugs as well. How can they let flies into a hospital? Stare at that cross on the wall. See the edges fuzzy and strobing – that's the drugs doing that. Sear the throat. Sink the boat. There's not much good poetry to come out of a hospital. Hear patients doing the shuffle step down the hall.

All that's missing now is the damned coffin. I'd like the body just to be taken home. Propped up in the corner by the telly. Let it watch the goddamned Conservative convention. Feed it porridge and help it with its prayers. Teach it to be quiet when there were visitors. Speak only when spoken to. People can be put off by corpses. Skinny blue legs stuck into slippers. Cold in the night with a blanket for its lap and staring out the frost-lined window. Still I'd like to have some mourners. A steady stream of them coming and going with tears and tissues. Wonder can you still hire out mourners? That was a wonderful tradition. Must mention to Claudine. The need for a lot of mournful people. I really wouldn't mind being surrounded by suffering. As I go.

They can wash you without taking off the gown.

They can really do what they like with you.

Read your chart.

Make notes.

Make minute adjustments to your responses to pain.

And then it will be said that Mr. Nowlan expired peacefully in the midst of great lamentations.

B   I think about death
how could I not
after everything

   but I think about it
as little as possible
like a dog
barking in the night

   too many fields away
for anything
to be done

   trucks and cars passing make a low buzz on the pavement
the screens in the restaurant windows sag and billow at the bottoms
I step outside, the aluminum door clatters behind me
light a cigarette

slow breath in
ash and fire falling
we could all of us be

but things look good from here they do

A   The diagnosis is grim, grim
we drove out into the country
sat on a hill overlooking the sea
listened to the birds and the wind
the foghorns
and I counted seventeen shades of green.

A   I can't get rid of this image of myself as a corpse after the funeral, they just bring me home and keep me here instead of putting me in the ground. They feed me rice pudding and light things like oatmeal or cream of wheat. The dead don't eat heavy. There's a poem in it of course which is why I keep thinking of it. As soon as I use it that'll be the end of it. Set me up in front of the hockey game, or the Conservative Leadership Convention even better.

It's because we are resilient that we go on. Or maybe because we lack the ability to imagine anything else. This is what keeps us making toast, or shovelling sidewalks, instead of running around screaming in the streets. What if I do die though? I mean soon. What if I die soon? And I think I will. Will.

B   Heather lifted her bags into the rear seat. This is a story after all. About the big hand of God. How it came down. We tore out onto the highway. She pulled her hair back from her face. Everything ends in the dark she said. But not everything dies. I know that. At night nothing but dark outside my window now. But yellow moon. A nice touch.

Forty-nine years old. There are prizes.

A   Salvation

   Towards the end
   I was two men
   I was the one that did all that writing
   and I was the one that could see all the way to the horizon
   there was no stopping
   the things that I could see.

A   Hooves Beating Time

   Shuffled out of doors in my bathrobe
   into the snow
   towards the ambulance

   wouldn't allow the attendants to help me
   had said I would die with dignity
   did

B   Ministry

   I don't mean to alarm you
   it's not bad news
   and shouldn't be news at all

   it's our job, I guess
   to try and save each other
   and to do the best we can

as little harm
as possible
while we wait.

John told me he kept on hearing her voice even after she was
gone and
that's what love is I guess.

MAY 1975

Alden Nowlan
met Johnny Cash
in Fredericton
true story
and it is not
documented
exactly what was said
but both men
having been
demonized
sainted
and given up for dead
saved
and hammered out
I imagine
what was said,
it might have eaten
up the darkness
for a bit
what is recorded
is that before anything much of interest could happen
the Prince of Wales
entered
no kidding
and started to discuss
beards
he was growing one
and Alden's was prodigious
the only recorded words were regarding beards.
Charles: My mother doesn't approve, I'm afraid.
Alden: Well Sir, what mum does?

sorry I couldn't
have been there
if only to stop Charles
from elbowing his way
into the room
and preventing
any interesting words
but then
every poem

is an apology for something.

Acknowledgements

Michael Ondaatje for his unknowing advice and for inspiration on page 131. My publisher Beth Follett for ongoing support, wisdom and her fine array of courage. My agents Hilary McMahon and Chris Casuccio for some careful work in the corners. Michael Holmes and Anita Lahey for first publishing a selection of these pieces in *Arc* magazine. Mary Newberry, once again, because you're my girl. Sandra Ridley for perceptive readings of successive drafts of this work, which otherwise would not have been this work. Barry Dempster for some knowing advice. Timothy Findley for the early encouragement we all need. And Debbie for leaving space for all the ghosts. Thank you.

Howlin' Wolf (a brief section of Wolf explaining blues structure on "The London Sessions" gave me everything that I needed; *"I'm just showin' you how to do it...let's get on it."*)

"Recollections" by Miles Davis, "Abide With Me" by Thelonius Monk and John Coltrane, "Dark Was The Night – Cold Was The Ground" by Blind Willie Johnson, "The Devil Comes Quick" and "Eggyolk Moon" by John Carroll, "On The Sea of Galilee" by The Carter Family, "I Got It Bad and That Ain't Good" by Keith Jarrett, "Cafarro's Theme" by Bill Frisell, Ron Mills, Curtis Fowlkes and Eyvind Kang and a variety of numbers by Buck 65 were a constant accompaniment.

These voices came scary easy. Many thanks are due for that.

Apologies

In 1947 the great bluesman Blind Willie Johnson's Beaumont Texas house burned down. Johnson was unable to help himself, and his wife Angeline dragged him from the flames and out onto the front lawn. They were alone and impoverished at the time and forced to live in the ashes of their former home and in this they were, a religious man might say, not unlike any of us.

I wanted to end easy and happy, but the best I could do was hope
Wanted to end easy and happy, but the best I could do was hope.
And I'm sorry about that. After all, it's not over yet.

Kick the dark.

Notes on Sources

The section "once a woman appeared" on page 69 is adapted from *Cash, the Autobiography*.

The phrase "a conspiracy of wings" on page 36 is from *Somewhere On A Saskatchewan – North Dakota Highway (Two) – The Atlas E Missile Complex* by Sandra Ridley (a Puddle Leaflet published 2007 by Max Middle).

The title "the man comes around" is the title of a Cash penned song from *American IV* (American Records, 2002).

The "peckerwoods" section on page 82 is from Guggenheim (John Simon) Memorial Foundation fellowship application. *Supplementary Statement No. 1*. Alden Nowlan Papers Msc. #40.15.41. University of Calgary.

The section "It is now early morning, was a bad night. The motel room seems large. The morning sun has concentrated all the cigarette smoke so you can see it hanging in pillars or sliding along the ceiling like amoebae. In the bathroom, I wash the loose nicotine out of my mouth. I smell the smoke still in my shirt. *Swallow fire*" on page 88 (with the exception of the italicized line) is from Michael Ondaatje's *Collected Works of Billy the Kid*.

The phrase "Heather's body is a tool for opening me up though" on page 100 is a modification of a line from "After Ajax" in *Some Days I Think I Know Things – The Cassandra Poems* by Rhonda Douglas.

The A section on page 101 "I can laugh. I do laugh. I shall die of laughter." is excerpted from "The Mists," Nowlan's first published poem accepted by *The Gruntvig Review* in 1951, the same year Alden is eighteen and attempts, unsuccessfully, to enlist in the armed forces to fly planes over Korea.

Parts of the A section "Uncertain then Certain" on page 107 are excerpted and/or adapted from a letter by Alden Nowlan to John Drew. 18 October 1966. Alden Nowlan Papers #40.10.49.34. University of Calgary Library.

The A section "once I was out flying a kite" on page 114 is excerpted from a letter by Alden Nowlan to Fred Cogswell. 21 May 1963. Fiddlehead Papers, File 1961-1972 #53. Harriet Irving Library, University of New Brunswick, Fredericton.

The A section "universal love song" on page 114 is excerpted from a letter by Alden Nowlan to Fred Cogswell. 21 May 1963. Fiddlehead Papers, File 1961-1972 #53. Harriet Irving Library, University of New Brunswick, Fredericton.

The dialogue between Layton and Nowlan on page 124 is from *If I could turn and meet myself: The Life of Alden Nowlan*.

The A section "the diagnosis is grim, grim" on page 131 is excerpted from a letter by Alden Nowlan to Elizabeth Brewster. 29 June 1966. Alden Nowlan Papers #40.3.23.5. University of Calgary Library, Calgary.

Works Cited or Consulted

Carr, Patrick and Cash, John. *Cash, the Autobiography*. New York: Harper, 1998.

Cook, Gregory M. *Alden Nowlan: Essays on His Works*. Toronto: Guernica Editions, 2006.

Douglas, Rhonda. *Some Days I Think I Know Things – The Cassandra Poems*. Winnipeg: Signature Editions, 2008.

Nowlan, Alden. *Bread, Wine and Salt*. Toronto: Clarke, Irwin & Company, 1967.

Ondaatje, Michael. *The Collected Works of Billy the Kid*. Toronto: House of Anansi, 1970.

Ridley, Sandra. *Somewhere On A Saskatchewan – North Dakota Highway (Two) – The Atlas E Missile Complex*. Ottawa: a Puddle Leaflet published by Max Middle, 2007.

Steele, Apollonia and Tener, Jean F. *The Alden Nowlan Papers*. Calgary: The University of Calgary Press, 1992.

Toner, Patrick. *If I could turn and meet myself: The Life of Alden Nowlan*. Goose Lane Editions, 2000.

TARA RUTHERFORD-BLOUIN

Michael Blouin has been published in most Canadian literary magazines. His novel *Chase and Haven* (Coach House 2008) won the 2009 ReLit Award for Best Novel and was a finalist for the Amazon.ca First Novel Award. *I'm not going to lie to you* (Pedlar Press 2007) was shortlisted for the Lampman-Scott Award. He has been a finalist for the CBC Literary Awards and is a past winner of the Diana Brebner Award (*Arc* magazine) and the Lillian I. Found Prize for Poetry. He is represented by Westwood Creative Artists and can be found at www.wcaltd.com and at www.minor-poet.blogspot.com.